SKATEBOARDING

Andy Horsley • • • • • • • • • • •

Heinemann Library
Chicago, Illinois

© 2003 Reed Educational & Professional Publishing
Published by Heinemann Library,
an imprint of Reed Educational & Professional Publishing,
Chicago, Illinois

Customer Service 888-454-2279
Visit our website at www.heinemannlibrary.com

Designed by Celia Floyd
Originated by Universal
Printed in Hong Kong by Wing King Tong

07 06 05 04 03
10 9 8 7 6 5 4 3 2 1

Library of Congress Cataloging-in-Publication Data

Horsley, Andy.
  Skateboarding / Andrew Horsley.
      p. cm. -- (Radical sports)
Includes bibliographical references and index.
Summary: Provides an overview of skateboarding including technique, equipment, guidelines, resources, and safety concerns.
  ISBN 1-58810-625-X (HC) 1-4034-0106-3 (Pbk)
  1. Skateboarding--Juvenile literature. [1. Skateboarding.] I. Title.
II. Series.
  GV859.8 .H66 2002
  796.22--dc21
                                        2001004804

Acknowledgments

The author and publishers are grateful to the following for permission to reproduce copyright material: Andy Horsley for permission to reproduce all photographs except: pp. 8–9 Tudor Photography; p. 11a David Walker; and p. 11b KPT Power Photos.

Cover photograph reproduced with permission of Andy Horsley.

Every effort has been made to contact copyright holders of any material reproduced in this book. Any omissions will be rectified in subsequent printings if notice is given to the publisher.

Some words are shown in bold, **like this.** You can find out what they mean by looking in the glossary.

CONTENTS

A short history of skateboarding

Skateboarding began in California during the late 1950s. A group of bored surfers tried putting a surfboard on roller skate wheels, and created the first skateboard.

The earliest skateboards were crude and dangerous forms of transportation. Rattling steel wheels made the skateboards shake. These were soon replaced by wheels made from baked clay. In the early 1970s skateboard manufacturers developed the smooth **urethane** plastic wheels that are still used today.

This 1970s skateboarder is doing a kickturn.

Early skateboards looked like miniature wooden surfboards. These "old school" boards were made from wood, plastic, or even metal. They were designed just for cruising. In the late 1960s, the introduction of the kicktail, an upturned back end, allowed for new tricks to be invented. There were many changes to the shape of boards throughout the 1970s and '80s. Most modern boards are made from maple wood and have both a kicktail and an upturned nose.

Types of skateboarding

The two main types of skateboarding are street and ramp. Street skating takes place on the street and uses urban obstacles such as curbs, stairs, and **handrails.** This can be dangerous and is banned in some cities. However, many skateparks have streetcourses that resemble the urban landscape. Skateparks offer a safe place to practice and can introduce you to ramp skating. Ramps are also known as **halfpipes**, and are shaped like the letter "U." Ramps come in three sizes—mini, midi, and **vert,** which is vertical at the top.

Why skateboard?

Once you have stepped on a skateboard you will understand why so many people love it. Skateboarding is challenging and is always fun and exciting. As you begin to perfect tricks, you will become more and more addicted to this radical sport.

This skater is catching air off of a vert ramp.

THE SKATEBOARD

Boards come in various sizes and widths for different needs. There are several different types. Budget boards for beginners are sold in most sporting good stores. Professional boards are available in specialty skateboarding stores.

Cheaper budget boards

As a beginner, you just need a cheap skateboard to get used to its movement and basic maneuvers. These boards are made from plywood instead of maple, and the wheels tend to be of low quality plastic. The ride on these boards is not as smooth as it is on a professional board. However, using a budget board is the easiest and cheapest way to see if skateboarding is for you.

Truckbolts

Four truckbolts are tightened through the deck and into each truck. These should be tight for stability and a solid ride.

Bearings

Bearings help the wheels turn smoothly.

Griptape

This is a non-slip covering similar to sandpaper. It is on all skateboards and ensures that your feet stay exactly where you put them.

Professional skateboards

If you decide to take skateboarding further, you will need a professional skateboard, also known as a "set-up." They are called professional boards because the actual deck usually bears the name of a world-class skateboarder; this will be his or her signature model. All the parts of a pro skateboard are sold separately and can be assembled by someone working at the store.

TOP TIP

If you've been introduced to skateboarding by a friend or relative, it might be worth asking if they or someone they know has a used skateboard. Always ask an experienced skateboarder to try the board out for you.

Kicktail

The back of the skateboard is called the kicktail. It is upturned to give leverage.

Wheel

Wheels are made of **urethane** and will guarantee a smooth, fast ride. Each wheel has two spaces for bearings, one in each side.

Nose

The front of the skateboard is called the nose. It is slightly upturned.

Deck

The deck will be made from seven layers of quality maple wood glued and pressed together. It will have a glossy finish and quality graphics.

Trucks

Each truck consists of two parts; baseplates that attach to the board and the hanger that the wheels bolt onto.

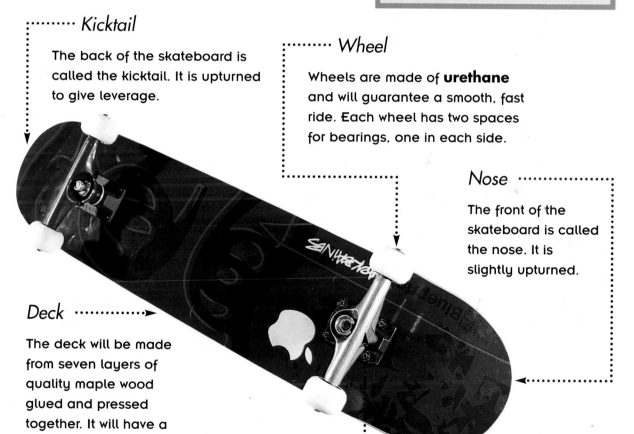

CLOTHES AND EQUIPMENT

As in all sports, you need to protect yourself from falls. Skateboarding has some special equipment that has been designed with your safety in mind. In addition to wearing the necessary protective pads, you should wear heavy clothing such as jeans and a long-sleeved shirt. Loose and baggy clothing is less restrictive, and will help you move freely.

Elbow pads

When you fall, it is best to try to roll out of it, in a ball-like shape protecting all of your extremities, such as arms and legs. Elbow pads help you take a rolling fall by protecting your elbows.

Knee pads

If you tumble off your board while skating you will probably fall on your knees. These plastic-capped pads will save your skin as well as your jeans.

Helmet

This is the most important piece of safety equipment. Made from hard plastic with a soft layer inside, the modern skate helmet is comfy and easy to wear. Unlike a bicycle helmet, it is designed to protect your head from multiple impacts. Many helmets now come with graphics printed onto them, so they look cool, too.

Wrist pads

These are essential for skateboarding. It is natural to put your arms out to save yourself when you fall. Wrist pads have sections of plastic that protect your wrists and save your palms from road rash.

Skate shoes

A lot of different companies make skateboarding shoes. These shoes are made of tougher materials than normal sports shoes. They will last a lot longer because they have tougher stitching and stronger soles.

Backpack

Carry a backpack stocked with skateboard survival equipment. Before you go anywhere, make sure that you pack a bottle of water to keep you from dehydrating. A good skate tool is also an essential item to bring in your backpack. If anything comes loose or falls off the board, you could be in for a long walk home if you cannot fix it. A block of wax will help some stubborn obstacles grind. And be sure to pack a box of bandages and an antiseptic in case you fall.

KEEPING FIT AND HEALTHY

Before you start skateboarding, it is important to get the blood flowing around your body and warm up the appropriate muscles.

Warming up

Skateboarding uses a lot of leg action, so a few leg stretches and some knee bending will be the best place to start. This will help move the blood to your knees, ankles, and thighs.

Body and arm stretches

These stretches will loosen up the rest of your body. Make sure that you keep your legs wide apart and as straight as you can. Touch the ground in front of you and then touch the toes on your right foot. Do this ten times and then repeat on the left foot.

Rotation of ankles

Skateboarding puts a lot of strain on your ankles, so before going out, do about 50 ankle rotations. Help your ankle to move by gently using your hands to spin and twist the foot (as if you were trying to take your feet off for the night). This will help your **ligaments** loosen up and reduce the risk of spraining, which would put a quick stop to the fun you're going to have!

Cooling down

To avoid getting stiff muscles after skating, you must cool down. Just jog on the spot or go for a quick walk. This will insure that you won't damage muscles or ligaments.

Nutrition

If you want to skate all day, the best way to keep your energy level up is to eat the right food. Carbohydrate-rich foods such as pasta, potatoes, and bread are good sources of energy. Drink plenty of water throughout the day to replenish your fluids, and maybe carry a few energy bars in your backpack to snack on.

Running helps you stay in shape.

Eating plenty of fresh vegetables helps to keep you healthy.

WHERE TO SKATE

There are different kinds of skateboard parks to visit, each with different obstacles.

Concrete

Concrete parks were popular in the 1960s and '70s and are now making a comeback. Concrete parks are like a smooth lunar landscape with dips and **bowls** to roll around on. Concrete is very smooth but also very fast, so take it easy.

Only use an outdoor skateboard park in good weather.

Wooden parks

Wooden parks are almost always indoors. You might have to pay a small fee to skate inside a park, but the money goes toward the upkeep of the obstacles. The obstacles might include **halfpipes** and mini-ramps (which are small halfpipes without **vert**), flat wooden banks, **quarterpipes**, **grind boxes,** and metal **handrails.** Most of the obstacles are built to simulate a real street environment.

You might enter your first competition in one of these indoor parks, so it's good to get comfortable with a few different ones if you can. Check with the owner and find out if any teams will be visiting to do demos or displays.

Outdoor skate ramps

Outdoor ramps are either metal or wood halfpipes ranging from mini-ramp to vert-ramp. These are only skateable when the weather is good. It is very dangerous to skate them at any other time.

Street skating

Sometimes you'll want to practice in a local park or an empty street, but street skating can be dangerous. It is now illegal to skate on some streets, so if you see any "No Skateboarding" signs you should find somewhere else to go. When you skate on the streets, make sure that you travel with a few friends so you will be in good hands if you **slam** or something happens.

Indoor wooden parks are fun, too!

SAFETY FIRST

- 🖐 Pay attention to other skaters.
- 🖐 Look out for wet surfaces.
- 🖐 Always wear full protective skate pads.
- 🖐 Be aware of your speed and direction.

THE BASICS

Are you goofy?

There are two ways to stand on a skateboard. You're either **goofy,** meaning you ride with your right foot forward, or **regular,** meaning you ride with your left foot forward. You will have to experiment to find out which is your riding **stance.** Try sliding across the kitchen floor in socks; whichever foot leads your slide will be the leading foot on the board. Or stand on your board in each stance and lean left and right and move around until you feel comfortable one way or the other.

Goofy and regular skateboarders battle it out on a mini-ramp.

Moving off

After finding the most comfortable stance, you will want to make your board move. Place your leading foot at the front of the board over the truck bolts—if your feet cover these bolts, your balance should be perfect. Use your back foot as a paddle to push the board along. When you and the board are moving, place the back foot over the back bolts. While you are moving, bend your knees and use your arms to help you balance. Stay over the board until it comes to a stop.

The tic-tac will keep you moving after you have pushed off. To tic-tac you lift the front wheels slightly off the ground and move the board to the left and to the right. This creates a sidewinder motion like a snake, which will move you forward.

Dropping off

When **dropping off** things such as small ledges or curbs, hold your feet over the truck bolts and keep your body weight and balance equal over the front and the back. Ride off the object keeping the board level by adjusting your balance. After the rear wheels have cleared the ledge, the board will touchdown onto the ground. Make sure all four wheels hit the ground at the same time, and bend your knees to absorb the impact.

Slowing down

If you feel you are moving too fast and you want to slow yourself down, take your back foot off the board and use the sole of your shoe as a brake, applying the bottom of your foot to the ground. You can also use this to stop. Another way to slow down is to lean back and use your back foot to press the tail down to the ground. You need to be more confident for this technique, and it will eventually wear out your board.

Stopping

The most obvious way to stop moving is to simply step off to the side and pick up your board. This will be all right while you are learning. As you gain confidence you can try more stylish ways to stop, including the most commonly used "step off and **grab.**" This involves taking the front foot off the board, placing it on the floor to the **heelside,** and propping the board up with the back foot, allowing you to pick the skateboard up by the nose.

Falling safely

There will be times when you will not be able to slow down or stop, so you need to know how to fall safely. A planned fall off the skateboard is called **bailing.**

The roll method

2. Make yourself into a ball. Be careful not to leave your hands and wrists sticking out.

1. When you feel you are about to fall off, step off the side of your board and perform a relaxed roll.

3. It is human nature to put your hands down first, but try to land on your side and roll away from the board.

The knee slide

Your knee pads will save you if you bail on a ramp. Fall to your knees, keeping them together. Then, **slide** down the ramp **transition** on your knees. Be aware of obstacles at all times, and use these techniques to avoid a **slam**— a hard, uncontrolled fall.

MORE TECHNIQUES

180 degree slide to fakie

Add a little spice to your routine by sliding the board around 180° to go backwards. This is called riding **fakie.**

As you are riding forward with your feet over the truck bolts, release some weight off your back foot and use it to push the back of the board around 180°—your front foot will act as a pivot.

Make sure that your body follows the board around until you and the board are moving backwards.

Skating transitions

Skating ramps is usually called skating **transitions.** Start at the top of the ramp with the tail of the skateboard held onto the **lip** with your back foot and the front of the skateboard sticking out over the ramp. Place your front foot over the front trucks and push off. Try to apply all four wheels to the ramp surface as soon as you can. Lean forward, but stay over the board and ride down the ramp.

Once you have dropped in you will soon reach the other side. In order to keep your speed, you have to work the transitions. This is called pumping. As you ride up the transition, thrust your body forward and up toward the lip; as you roll back down the transition, thrust downward and roll fast across the flat bottom of the ramp.

Turning (carving)

After you have practiced this for a while you can start to learn turning, or **carving.** Apply weight and pressure to either the **toeside** or the **heelside** of the board. If you lean toeside, you will make the board turn inward **(backside).** Leaning heelside will turn the board outward **(frontside).**

1. Roll up the transition.

Kickturning

Kickturns are needed to turn around on a ramp. Backside kickturns are usually the easiest ones to do.

2 + 3. When you are close to the top of the ramp (the lip), lift the front wheels slightly and carve your body and board around to face back down the transition.

4. Place all four wheels back on the ramp and ride down.

THE OLLIE

The ollie is the basis for nearly all of the skateboard tricks that you can think of. This trick has been around since the late 1970s and was invented by a skateboarder named Alan "Ollie" Gelfand. The ollie is basically a jump, but it is very important to learn. It will have you pulling your hair out for a while, but if you stick with it, you will be having fun for years to come.

This is where the curved ends of your skateboard come into play. The upturned tail of your skateboard is the key to the ollie. Pulling off a good ollie is all in the timing, so practice is important. Start learning this trick moving very slowly. It requires that you move your back foot away from the safety of the truck bolts and rest the toes in the center of the tail. Your front foot can stay over the front truck bolts.

This skater demonstrates the ollie grab.

The trick consists of seven steps:
1. As you ride along with your back foot toes in the center of the tail, bend your knees as if to power up your legs for a big jump.
2. Using your back foot, hit the tail down hard on the ground. (In order to do this you must take weight off the front foot by bending the knee.) The board will tip up backwards.

3. As the tail hits the ground, you must jump up, sliding your front foot along the griptape toward the end of the nose.
4. This scraping will pull the board up. Your back foot should leave the board so that the back end of the skateboard can take off as well.
5. You will have jumped taking the skateboard with you. Level out your feet and board and prepare to return to the ground.
6. As you touchdown, your feet should be back over the truck bolts for perfect stability and balance.
7. Ride away with a smile on your face!

Perfecting the ollie requires a lot of practice.

The ollie is THE trick to learn if you want to take skateboarding any further than just moving, but it takes a lot of time and patience to learn.

Now that you understand the ollie, here are a few tricks that use it.

Grinds

The section of your truck in between the wheels is the **grinding** area. Grinds are when your trucks come into contact with a surface and you travel on the trucks instead of the wheels. Grinds can be done on curbs, ramp **coping, grind boxes,** or **handrails.**

Basic 50-50 grind

A 50-50 grind is when you ollie onto an object and grind both trucks along the obstacle. The thing to remember about grinds is to go fast and keep your weight over the trucks.

Boardslides

Boardslides are **sliding** along a block, rail, or ramp coping using the belly of the board to slide. No contact is made by the wheels. Move with your toes forward, balancing on the board's middle. This takes a lot of practice and a lot of balance, but it feels great when you have mastered it.

Balance and skill are needed to perform a long 50-50 grind such as this.

Nose and tailslides

To do a noseslide, ollie up onto the nose and slide along an obstacle on the tip of the board. Apply pressure to the nose to help the board slide along the obstacle.

A backside tailslide requires a lot of practice.

The tailslide is pretty much the same. Instead of using the front end of the board to slide, you use the tail. Apply pressure and forward momentum to help the tail slide.

Wheelies

This is a simple trick that will help you perfect your balance. The nose of the board is held up above the ground while the back wheels are rolling along. Ollie up onto platforms, landing in a wheelie position. Ride along on the back wheels for as long as you can.

Kickflips

The kickflip is what most skaters want to learn first but this move definitely comes after the ollie has been mastered. A kickflip is when the board is kicked with the front foot, making the board flip around. It spins around 360° and lands with all four wheels back down on the pavement. Many hours will be spent learning this trick, and even with years of practice it will still be difficult to pull off.

Your skateboard should be checked often so you will have a smooth and safe ride every time. Here are a few things that you should check regularly.

Wheels

Wheels tend to cone outward after a while. This means that they wear down on the outer edge. To fix this, take the wheels off, turn them around and replace them. The wheels will even out as you skate.

Bearings

Bearings can become rusted and squeaky, especially if you have ridden through water. Some bearings can be dismantled and cleaned.

Make sure the wheels are tight at all times. You do not want them to fall off!

This is a tricky job. Bearings should be cleaned with a spray lubricant (oil) and then greased. Sometimes the ball bearings have been damaged. You will have to replace the damaged bearings with new ones.

Truck bushings

Truck bushings are the two rubber blocks that rest between the hanger and the baseplate. They can split after a while, but they are inexpensive and can breathe some life into old, worn-out trucks.

Trucks

Trucks will last a long time, maybe even years. The baseplates sometimes snap, but you can buy those separately.

Kingpin

The kingpin is the bolt that holds the hanger of the truck onto the baseplate. It can snap if it is stressed. These are cheap to replace, but you will have to take the whole truck off to change it.

Griptape

Griptape can sometimes become blocked with dirt and lose its grip. Gently wash the griptape with a damp sponge and dry the water off with a kitchen towel. If that does not help, you can replace the damaged griptape.

You can buy various skate tools that will contain all of the right size sockets and screwdriver heads. Some are small and specialized, and some come with a few different attachments. The best ones usually come with everything attached, so you will not lose the different parts.

This is a typical skate tool.

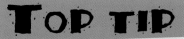

TOP TIP

🖐 Take care of your board and try not to take it out in wet weather. It is bad for your deck and can also be dangerous. Leave the water to the surfers!

TAKING IT FURTHER

Skateboard competitions and events are held around the world almost every weekend. Some of these events feature skateboarding stars going crazy. Others are for young, up-and-coming amateur skaters. These events are advertised in skateboard magazines and in skateboard stores. They offer a chance to see your heroes in action, or practice your skills.

There are two main categories in a skateboard competition—**vert** ramp riding and street style.

Vert ramp riding

Vert riding is another name for skating a vertical skateboard ramp. This is spectacular to watch and is often the way that skateboarding is first encountered. The vert competition consists of each rider doing as many tricks as he or she can without falling off during a 45-second run. They are judged on the technical difficulty of their runs. Sometimes there is a "highest air" category in the vert competition. This is a real crowd pleaser. Skaters jump as high as they can out of the top of the ramp and then land back in again.

This skater is competing in a vert ramp riding competition.

Street style

A huge section of the arena where the skate competition is held will be devoted to replicating obstacles and objects that you would find on a real street or in a parking lot. The street area is where you will see the most incredible tricks being tried and some awesome trick combinations attempted. There is always a "best trick" prize at the end of a street competition.

Sponsorship

Being sponsored is nice. It means getting free skateboard gear, and maybe even being paid to skate. That said, sponsorship should never be chased. As you become more and more confident at skating, you will want to enter competitions and might eventually achieve high rankings. This is a good way of being seen and getting your name around the skate circuit. Always remember there will be many other skaters out there hoping for the same thing. If you have the talent (and a little bit of luck) the sponsorship will come to you. Just have fun skateboarding for yourself.

This skater is doing a boardslide at the street area of an arena.

Skateboarders can be found in every country. Many skaters travel to different countries to do demonstrations and enter competitions. Some of them have become famous all over the world.

Tony Hawk

Tony is the most famous skater alive. He even has his own video game and clothing line. Tony was the first person to land a 900 at the X Games—that is 2 1/2 full spins out of the top of the ramp. He can also skate a full loop, skateboarding upside down around a fullpipe— a full circle of wood, concrete, or metal.

Bob Burnquist

Bob learned to skate on very poorly maintained skateparks in Brazil. He is one of the world's most talented **vert** ramp riders. Bob is known for his switchstance skating abilities. This means he can ride using both **stances.**

Tony Hawk is so good on a vert ramp that people have started to build special ramps just for him. These have enormous gaps to jump and other death-defying obstacles built-in.

Eric Koston

Eric was born in Thailand but moved to California when he was young. He is considered the biggest star in street skating. Eric has the ability to string together very technical tricks. He has made sponsorship money by promoting a popular skateboard shoe.

Elissa Steamer

Elissa Steamer has been skateboarding since she was twelve and she turned professional in 1998. Since then, she has risen through the ranks of professional skateboarding to stand among some of the best skaters in the world.

Tom Penny

Tom grew up skateboarding on the streets in England. When he moved to the U.S., everyone noticed how confident he was. Tom can do tricks and skate vert with the same ease and precision. This makes him one of the most well-rounded skaters around.

Tom Penny cops huge air.

GLOSSARY

backside turn or move with your back facing outward and your toes facing inward

bailing to leave your skateboard before you crash; not to be confused with slamming

bowl concrete skatepark obstacle that looks like an empty swimming pool; usually made from smooth concrete, but wooden bowls are sometimes found in indoor parks

carve to turn the board at high speed without sliding on the wheels, usually on a ramp or bank

coping top edge or lip of a ramp, bowl, or block; made from metal tubing on ramps

drop off to ride off something involving a drop, such as a curb or block

fakie riding backwards

frontside turn with your chest facing outward and heels facing inward

goofy standing with your right foot on the front of the skateboard, pushing with your left foot

grab where you grab the board during a trick

grind riding along the truck's surface rather than the wheels

grind box box or block with an edge or coping that you can grind along

halfpipe big "U"-shaped tube with a flat bottom, usually made from wood but sometimes concrete or metal

handrails metal handrails that go down stairs

heelside side of the board closest to the inside of your heel (right for goofy stance, left for regular)

ligaments tough bands of elastic tissue that hold joints together

lip top edge of a ramp or bowl

quarterpipe half of a halfpipe; one transition or one curve

regular standing with your left foot on the front of the skateboard, pushing with your right foot

slamming hard uncontrolled or unexpected fall

slide to slide on parts of the deck; to slide on the knees to avoid injury

stance position you stand on a board, either goofy or regular

toeside the side of the board closest to your toe (left for goofy stance, right for regular)

transition the curve or bend of a ramp

urethane high-quality plastic used for making wheels

vert jump ramp that has a vertical section at the top

USEFUL ADDRESSES

United Skateboarding Association
(USA)
P.O. Box 986
New Brunswick, NJ 08903

International Gravity Sports
Association (IGSA)
638 N. Crestview Drive
Glendora, CA 91741

Skatepark Association of the
United States of America
2118 Wilshire Blvd. #622
Santa Monica, CA 90403

MORE BOOKS TO READ

Horsley, Andy. *Skateboarding.* Austin, TX : Raintree Steck-Vaughn
Publishers, 2001.

Peterson-Kaelberer, Angie. *Skateboarding Greats: Champs of the
Ramps.* Minnetonka, MN: Capstone Press, Inc., 2002.

Wingate, Brian. *The Complete Book of Skateboards and Skateboarding
Gear.* New York, NY: Rosen Publishing Group, 2002.

INDEX